W9-AVM-963

# Spin Again

## Board Games from the Fifties and Sixties

**Rick Polizzi & Fred Schaefer**

**Photography by Rick Polizzi**

Chronicle Books · San Francisco

Copyright 1991 by Chronicle Books. All rights reserved. No part of this book may be reproduced
without written permission from the Publisher.

Cover design: Brenda Rae Eno and
Merrick Mae Hamilton

Typesetting by Wilsted & Taylor, Oakland,
California

Printed in Hong Kong.

Library of Congress Cataloging-in-
Publication Data
Polizzi, Rick.
    Spin again : Board games from the fifties and
sixties / by Rick Polizzi and Fred Schaefer ;
photography by Rick Polizzi.
        p.   cm.
    ISBN 0-87701-830-8 (pbk.)
    1. Board games—United States—History.
I. Schaefer, Fred.   II. Title.
GV1312.P65   1991
794—dc20                          91-8343
                                    CIP

Milton Bradley games used with permission of Milton
Bradley Company, a subsidiary of Hasbro, Inc.

Mattel games used with permission of Mattel, Inc.

Photograph of The Checkered Game of Life courtesy of
The National Museum of American History, Smithsonian
Institution. Not to be reproduced without permission of
the Smithsonian Institution.

Use of all trademarked terms or logos is in no way
to be construed as detracting from their trademark
status. All rights herein reserved by their respective
manufacturers.

Distributed in Canada by Raincoast Books,
112 East Third Avenue, Vancouver, B.C. V5T 1C8

10   9   8   7   6   5   4   3   2   1


Chronicle Books
275 Fifth St.
San Francisco, CA 94103


If you like the book, you'll love the club! Join **Spin
Again,** featuring a quarterly newsletter chock-
full of toys and games from the past forty years:

**Spin Again**
12210 Nebraska Avenue
Los Angeles, CA 90025

**Dedicated to
Richard Emery Polizzi**

To the many people in the toy industry who took the time to talk to us at length about this unique period in American games, or who simply pointed us in the right direction, our sincere thanks:

Julie Cooper, Jim Houlihan, Mel Taft, Larry Reiner, Harold Frankel, Reuben Klamer, Bea Pardo, Ralph Pereida, Sid Sackson, Lionel Weintraub, Randolph P. Barton, Bill Dohrman, Roy Raizen, Jerry Goldstein, Morton A. Simon, Mr. and Mrs. Leroy Fadem, Joe Wetherell, Bill Hill, Jack McMann, Bob Fisher, Diane Cardinale at Toy Manufacturers of America, Robert Bohnenberger, Nick Agneta, David Kaplinsky, Kent Salisbury, George Hoehne, Jerry Houle, Bruce Whitehill, and Marvin Silbermintz.

Thanks are also due to:
Don Wilmoth, who shared his Western collection, Tony Kirsch, owner of Stuff Mom Threw Out in New Orleans, Paul Fink, Bill Hughes, Alfonzo Smith, Bill Longstreet and his newsletter *The Name of the Game* (P.O. Box 721, Plainville, CT 06062), Scott James, Neal Miller, Laura Coplen, Joe Romero, Steve Fadem, Bob Barrett, Leon Janzen, Rob Bender, Tom Wilson, Robert Borowski, Cal Beauregard, and Joedi Johnson.

And to everyone at Chronicle Books:
Nion McEvoy, who gave us the "green light"; Charlotte Stone, who juggled last-minute details; and our art director, Karen Pike, and Brenda Eno.

Friends contributed in numerous ways, offering encouragement or practical advice. Thanks to:
Jim Belcher for his generous photographic advice; Betsey Binet for her sharp yet gracious editorial skills; Churchill Films of Los Angeles; Kevin Radecker for making the first phone call; our agent, Peter Miller; and our parents, Richard and Madeline Polizzi, and Fred and Helen Schaefer, who made it all possible by giving us a ton of games when we were kids.

In addition, Fred would like to thank Ann Wills, who sacrificed an entire vacation day doing research for us, and Chris Hofland for his persistent encouragement.

Finally, special thanks to Carla Polizzi for her 24-hour devotion to the project, without whom we could never have pulled this off.

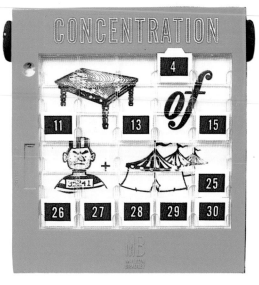

*Mansion of Happiness,* W. & S. B. Ives, 1843

In 1923, archaeologist Howard Carter wiped his brow and pried open the tomb of Tutankhamen. His anticipation of discovering perhaps the archaeological find of the century, and the fame and riches that would follow, led him farther into the dark, silent catacomb. Once there, he found gold, jewelry, precious artifacts—and a game board, complete with dice and playing pieces. A game played by Egyptian royalty! If he had never found his way out of that stone labyrinth, at least he wouldn't have been bored.

Generations later, in neighborhoods across America, suburban archaeologists are rolling up their sleeves, prying open their attics, and braving dust and cobwebs in search of more elusive treasures: the games they played when they were young.

## A Brief History of Playing

Humans have cultivated the art of playing for thousands of years. The Egyptians, Greeks, and Romans enjoyed, in varying forms, backgammon, checkers, dominoes, and chess. Elaborate dolls and other toys have turned up in the coffins of Roman children, while one Greek vase sports a picture of a young boy playing with a yo-yo, a toy that eventually vanished in Europe only to reappear in the late 18th century as an import from the Far East. It seems you can't keep a good fad down.

Board games have existed for over 4,000 years. They were enjoyed in the Western Hemisphere before Columbus and his sea-crazed crew stumbled on the New World.

When the first European settlers arrived in North America they brought with them their children's games and toys to use for bartering with the presumably entertainment-starved "savages" and, perhaps, to remind themselves of a world left behind. Some toys, however, probably were carted across the gray Atlantic simply to quiet the piercing screams of stubborn children.

Although survival in the American wilderness left little time for playing, the settlers did manage to learn from the Native Americans (who, it turned out, already knew how to have a good time) the art of creating toys and games from basic materials. Corncobs became dolls, balls were fashioned from rawhide, and dried corn kernels made fine game tokens.

It wasn't until after the American Revolution that the first toy companies appeared in the States, and still another century elapsed before the emergence of today's legendary manufacturers.

Typically, many game companies began as stationery, lithography, or bookselling businesses whose founders quickly saw the merits of "publishing" board games. Since games at the time were made entirely of paper and cardboard, it was a natural progression for these companies.

In 1843, the W. & S. B. Ives Company, a well-respected stationer in Salem, Massachusetts, produced the first American board game, Mansion of Happiness, in which good deeds led children and their playing pieces down the path to "eternal happiness." Invented by Anne W. Abbott, the daughter of a clergyman, the game was designed to promote morality and good values, a trend that would become popular in future games. Frivolous game-playing was apparently condoned in Puritan households only if the fun and laughs led you straight down the path of righteousness.

Many years later, in Springfield, Massachusetts, a young man by the name of Milton Bradley was looking for something to invigorate his ailing lithography business. In 1860 he printed The Checkered Game of Life. Like Mansion of Happiness, Bradley's game was meant to instill morality in children by rewarding good deeds and punishing bad ones. The first player to reach "Happy Old Age" was the winner. The game was an

immediate success, selling over 45,000 copies during its first year of release.

The fledgling American toy and game industry thrived until the outbreak of the Civil War, when imports were scuttled and business hit a lull. Immediately following the war, toy sales boomed once more. By 1900, over 500 toy companies competed for sales estimated at $20 million. "Playing" had suddenly become serious business.

In February 1902, ten sales representatives from American toy factories set up temporary headquarters in a Lower Manhattan hotel for four weeks. Their goal: to entice professional buyers with new American toys and games. The practice became so successful that other salespeople followed suit, making it an annual affair in New York City. Thus began the American

International Toy Fair, today one of the largest toy trade shows in the United States.

Later, Toy Fair was managed by the Toy Manufacturers of America, the industry's trade association, founded in 1916. TMA was and still is "the voice of the U.S. toy industry to government, trade, the media and consumers."

At Toy Fair, manufacturers introduce their new product lines to buyers from the major toy store chains and jobbers who purchase products for the smaller independent businesses. There, toy companies get their first hint of an item's future popularity. If buyers don't think a game will do well, they are hesitant to submit large orders. Toy Fair is also a good place to

anticipate future trends by getting a peek at where other companies are heading with their product lines. It's that little edge that counts in the highly competitive world of toys and games.

## Fads and Trends

Board games have always mirrored our society, reflecting our customs, culture, and some of the more mundane aspects of our lives. Regardless of current trends or fads, game manufacturers realized early on that if a game wasn't challenging and fun, it would simply sit on the toy store shelves—a disaster for any game company.

    The sermonlike morality games of the 1800s were popular because they embodied the deep-rooted religious values of the community. The family that plays together—well, let's just say these types of

*Game of Round the World with Nellie Bly,*
McLoughlin Bros., 1890

**A Trip Around the World,** *Parker Bros., ca. 1920s*

*Innocence Abroad,* Parker Bros., 1888

games were popular because it was the *parents* who bought them. Eventually, morality games began to wane and were replaced by games that reflected a wider variety of American interests.

For instance, in the late 1800s, travel became more accessible due to lower fares and improved traveling conditions. More Americans traveled abroad, and when they returned, they could relive their trip through Milton Bradley's 1873 travel game Around the World, or the McLoughlin Brothers' 1890 Game of Round the World with Nellie Bly. Travel games remained popular in the 1900s; one such example is Parker Brothers' A Trip Around the World (ca. 1920).

The publishing world also had a direct effect on board games. What made popular reading, game inventors reasoned, could become popular game playing. When Mark Twain's *The Innocents Abroad* was published, George S. Parker created a travel board game loosely based on it, Innocence Abroad. The game began to attract so much public attention that Parker decided to advertise his game in newspapers and magazines, an unprecedented practice at the time.

History, sports, inventions, comics, even politics influenced games. One such political game, Balance the Budget, introduced in 1938, advertised on its box cover, "Democrats, Republicans, even Congressmen are playing it!" (Perhaps today's politicians could learn a thing or two from this pastime.) But none of these trends had as much impact on the game industry as the advent of television.

## The Fifties and Sixties

Between 1948 and 1958, Americans spent over $15 billion on television sets. As television infiltrated the national psyche, game companies worried that this new "toy" would edge out family game-playing. Little did they realize how revolutionary and positive it would be for the toy industry: inspiring board games and offering an entirely new forum for reaching their true customers (kids!) directly by advertising during their favorite programs.

One of the first television personalities to lend his likeness to a board game was Hopalong Cassidy. In the early fifties and well into the sixties, TV Westerns were immensely popular with adults as well as children. In 1949, James J. Shea, then president of the Milton Bradley Co., believed that television could actually encourage game-playing. So when he heard that the popular television cowboy had received a hero's welcome from his fans in New York, Shea immediately arranged a meeting with Hopalong. Shea returned home with permission to create a Hopalong Cassidy game, the first of many television tie-ins for Milton Bradley. This began a trend that spread to all the major game companies.

The Vietnam War may have been partly responsible for the popularity of war toys during the sixties. Included among them were war *games*. These war-related products for children eventually aroused the passion of parents' groups concerned about the psychological effect "war-gaming" had on their children. They believed that toy weapons and war games glorified war and desensitized children to the suffering and devastation of real warfare. The Vietnam combat footage that was beamed into their homes nightly on the evening news was bad enough, they reasoned; they didn't want their children to spend all day pretending to be killing machines. These parents' groups became increasingly active and had a perceptible effect upon the toy industry, and by 1966, war toys were on the decline.

As kids became more sophisticated and demanding in their entertainment, they created a market for three-dimensional games that combined the goal-oriented play of board games and the visual fun of mechanical action toys. In some ways, three-dimensional action games were visual precursors to the video games of the seventies. Suddenly, the typical flat game board was simply too humdrum for the revolutionary game-players of the sixties. Visual stimulus would become a crucial part of any successful game.

It wasn't until the launch of the first *real* satellite, the Soviet Union's Sputnik in 1957, that the public finally embraced outer-space merchandise. Suddenly, space exploration was no longer a fantasy; it was necessary for the very survival of our country. Subsequent NASA space missions supplied some real-life heroes to fuel our imaginations: *astronauts*. Now, blasting off into the great unknown was the patriotic thing to do. And how could Mom object to that? Besides, these new "space men" were so clean-cut and handsome.

**Hopalong Cassidy,** *Milton Bradley, 1950*

Why, they could be your next-door neighbors.

Activity games were in vogue with adults as well as children in the sixties. People were socializing more, getting in touch with their feelings (as well as their neighbors' feelings), and enjoying group activities that included these appropriate "party games."

Looking back on our social history, it's clear that the fifties and sixties were two of the most colorful and turbulent decades in American history. They were landmark decades that couldn't have been more different, yet it's easy to see how one grew out of the other. Like all memorabilia, board games reflect our cultural similarities and differences, giving us a glimpse of the nation: our dreams, shortcomings, and achievements.

**Men Into Space,** *Milton Bradley, 1960*

## Spin Again—

American board games have entertained, educated, and inspired for over a century and a half. In many ways, our childhoods are defined by the games we played. There is a certain camaraderie present when we stumble onto someone who owned and played the same games we did. Soon we're discussing what we loved or hated about particular games—features that didn't work properly, rules that were changed or broken to make the game more fun—and, finally, reluctantly admitting that when *we* were winning, it seemed to be a game of skill, but when our opponent was ahead, it was obviously a game of luck.

We fondly remember the games we played because they were *our* games, our universe away from parents, teachers, and the real world that was rapidly closing in on us. Games were something to call our own.

Now, in a world that seems to be growing out of control, we're rediscovering the art of playing.

It's time to spin again.

## DON'T TOUCH THAT DIAL!

Nothing had a greater effect on the toy industry than the introduction of that flickering box into American living rooms. As television gained a stronghold in American life, game companies realized that if kids (and their parents) faithfully watched a television program once a week, then perhaps they would play a game based on it the other six days.

Thus began the days of the large licensing companies, who merchandised television shows to the toy industry. Basically, a license grants permission to manufacture a toy or a game (or anything, really) based on fictional characters or real people. The practice be-

came so popular and profitable for the toy industry that television licenses were being offered and bid on by companies even before the programs were broadcast. The game people suddenly found themselves playing the role of network executives, speculating on what the next hit television show would be.

Product inspiration aside, television also opened up a whole new arena for the game manufacturers' marketing departments. Before the 1950s, they relied on word of mouth to create a hit board game. The only advertising open to them was print ads in newspapers and magazines, and those were aimed specifically at mothers, the predominant purchasers of games for their children. But with the television invasion, game company executives realized that they could now reach their audience directly. Unfortunately, this created as much controversy as profits. Parents began to voice their objections to toy advertisements on television.

"The toy industry was unmercifully attacked by parents' groups who accused us of turning their children into monsters!" says Mel Taft, who was an executive at Milton Bradley for 35 years. "If children saw a game advertised on television and wanted it, they could make life miserable for their parents. Consequently, the industry got some bad publicity for television advertising. Really, their main gripe was that advertising to kids was wrong because if kids wanted something, they'd get it!"

Controversy aside, the marriage of television and the toy industry brought televisionland to the kitchen table. Suddenly, it wasn't Dad sitting across the table, but Napoleon Solo, the man from U.N.C.L.E. Or, on another day, he could be Ben Casey, M.D., surgeon *extraordinaire*. And was that Mom rolling the dice or a "Bewitched" Samantha Stephens one space away from turning Uncle Arthur into a chimp?

*Actor Bob Crane takes time off on the set of "Hogan's Heroes" to inspect Transogram's newest game, Hogan's Heroes Bluff Out.*

**Today with Dave Garroway,** *Athletic Products Co., 1950's "Today Show" viewers got a glimpse of the studio and how to run it in this beautiful three-dimensional game. The playing pieces were tiny metal television cameras.*

The James Bond movies were such a hit that Milton Bradley released several games based on the Ian Fleming character.

**My Fair Lady,** Standard Toykraft, 1963
**How to Succeed in Business Without Really Trying,** Milton Bradley, 1963
Although both titles were made into movies, these games were released a year earlier, based on the hit musicals.

Television game shows also inspired a string of board games. Although "home versions" of popular game shows have generally sold very well, some companies were hesitant to produce them at first, fearing their customers would rather play along with the television show than purchase the game.

One such example was Milton Bradley's reluctance to release the game Concentration. Company executives were concerned that fans of the television show were only interested in the program. After all, Concentration was popular in part because of its celebrity host, Hugh Downs. When the family opened Milton Bradley's game version, there would be no lovable host to provide laughs and console the losers. Ultimately, it didn't matter, the game was a best-seller (with Milton Bradley issuing many editions over the years), and television-game-show board games were, and still are, well loved.

By the sixties, television, although still immensely popular, had begun to lose some of its novelty. Like the radio, it had become a piece of furniture. Suddenly, moviegoing was an event again. The movie theater was somewhere to go with your date. It was a way to get out of the house, away from Mom and Dad. Also, theaters offered more exotic and risqué fare than the family entertainment that dominated network television.

The mid-sixties ushered in an enormous spy craze, thanks to a chap by the name of James Bond. In 1966, roughly two dozen spy movies were released, and network television offered at least ten spy-related shows. Besides whetting our appetite for toy weapons and spy gadgets, these heroes infiltrated the game world, producing several card and board games.

A few game companies looked to New York City for inspiration, nabbing some hot Broadway musicals: *How to Succeed in Business Without Really Trying* (the first musical to be used as the basis of a board game) and the hit musical *My Fair Lady.*

The image of Americans as industrious, hard-working individuals, born of the work ethic, belies an essential element of our character: we *crave* entertainment. From radio and television to motion pictures and plays, we pursue leisure with a vengeance—and once we've grasped it, we don't want it to end. Of course, it doesn't have to, for our favorite characters, heroes, and programs have traditionally found new life on a game board.

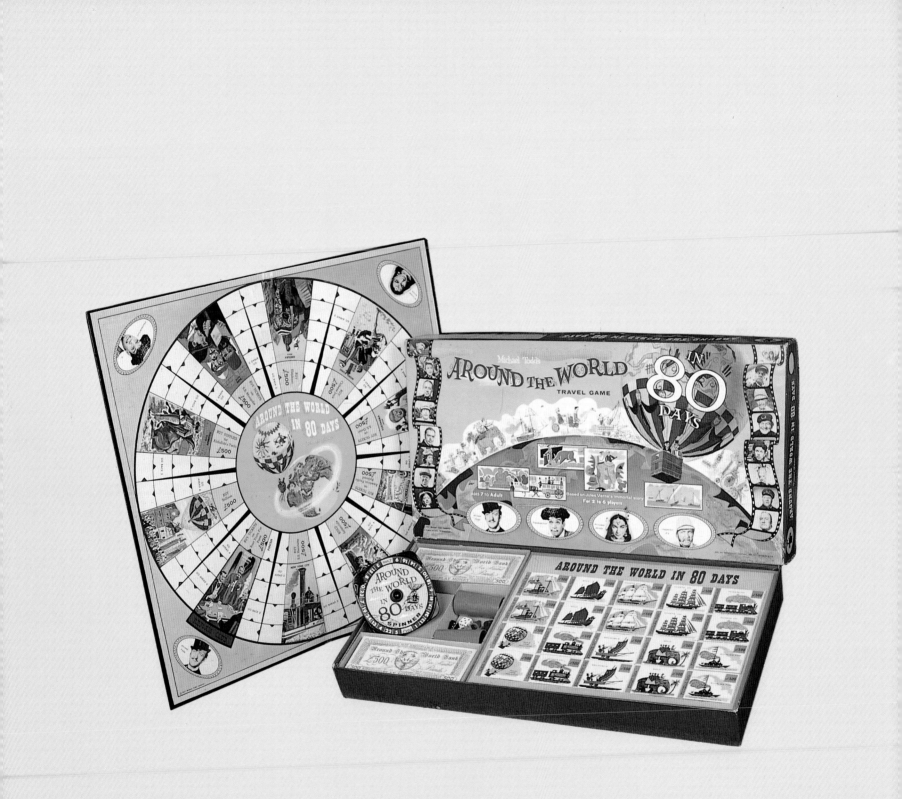

**Around the World in 80 Days,** *Transogram, 1957*
*Hollywood took on Jules Verne with this Michael Todd epic starring David Niven as Phileas Fogg.*

***Jackie Gleason's "And Awa-a-a-a-y We Go!" TV Fun Game,*** *Transogram, 1956*
*Players assumed the role of famous Gleason characters—Joe the Bartender, Fenwick Babbit, Ralph Kramden—and went in search of the perfect script, winning the game by getting the most "laffs."*

**Phil Silvers Sgt. Bilko,** *Gardner Games, 1955*
*Beat the brash loud-mouthed Bilko at his own game.*

**I'm George Gobel,** *Schaper, 1955*
*Old Lonesome George's comedy show was tops for several years, and the board game is full of "Gobelisms," the sayings he made popular: "Well, I'll be a dirty bird!"*

**Land of Giants,** *Ideal, 1968*
Set in the future (1983), this game is based on the Irwin Allen TV show about a group of space castaways who found themselves in a strange land where everything was 12 times larger than on Earth.

**Bewitched,** *Game Gems, 1965*
All Darrin and Samantha wanted was to get to Vacationland, but then along came Endora—

**Gilligan's Island,** *Game Gems, 1964*
They could have retitled this game Three Men and a Monkey, since it's missing four of the castaways.

**McHale's Navy,** *Transogram, 1962*
McHale and his men try to outmaneuver each other in PT boats around the Island of Taratupa.

**Gomer Pyle,** *Transogram, 1964*
According to the rules, "each player, as Gomer, races about placing his men in any willy-nilly formation for a grand salute to Sergeant Carter on his birthday." Artist Hal Greer shows the irascible Sergeant Carter chewing out the "green" Marine.

**F Troop,** *Ideal, 1965*

**Time Tunnel,** *Ideal, 1966*
A top-secret government experiment gone wrong flings two young scientists into any historical or futuristic situation imaginable. Kids who played this game probably lost all sense of time.

**Candid Camera,** *Lowell, 1963*
Just when you least expect it, someone, somewhere, puts out a board game based on a show you never dreamed could be turned into one.

**Captain Gallant,** *Transogram, 1955*
Former Tarzan and Olympic Gold Medalist Buster Crabbe and his son Cullen starred as Foreign Legionnaires in this adventure series shot entirely in Morocco.

**I Spy,** Ideal, 1965
**Man from U.N.C.L.E.,** Ideal, 1965

**My Favorite Martian,** Transogram, 1963
Earthling Bill Bixby with his Martian sidekick Ray Walston starred in this way-out series.

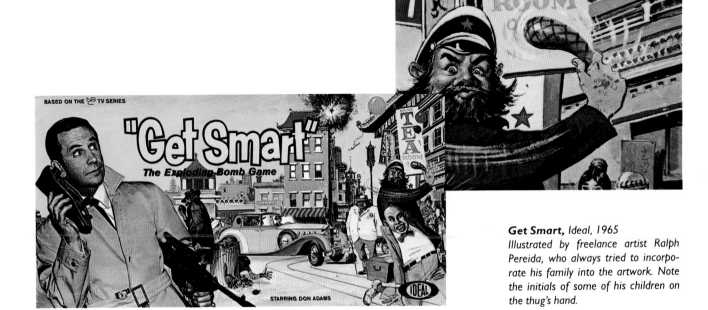

**Get Smart,** Ideal, 1965
Illustrated by freelance artist Ralph Pereida, who always tried to incorporate his family into the artwork. Note the initials of some of his children on the thug's hand.

**Shenanigans,** *Milton Bradley, 1964*
A case where the television program and the board game were designed simultaneously. To advertise their own games, Milton Bradley created a game show for kids hosted by Stubby Kaye.

*Opposite page:*
**Masquerade Party,** *Bettye B, 1955*
Famous people were disguised in costumes and a celebrity panel had to deduce who they were through clues. By the way, the three figures in the foreground are (from left to right) comedian George Jessel, polar explorer Admiral Byrd, and light-heavyweight boxing champ Maxie Rosenbloom.

Aunt Ida needs new bed and special mattress.

**$200**

An exciting Quiz Game that captures all the thrills of the popular TV Show!

*Sponsored by*
COLGATE—PALMOLIVE COMPANY

for Children and Adults

# STRIKE IT RICH

*with* WARREN HULL

ON TV COAST-TO-COAST

Aunt Jane needs money for liver operation.

**$400**

Daddy

**Strike It Rich,** *Lowell, 1956*
*On this quiz show, hard-luck contestants tried to answer questions for cash. Those who lost went to the "Heart Line," where viewers called in to donate money or gifts.*

**Twenty-One,** *Lowell, 1956*
*The 1958 quiz show scandals busted this game show. It was exposed that the producers were feeding the correct answers to those contestants who were more likely to appeal to the American public. Lowell's version included two "soundproof" booths, each with an automatic calculator.*

*Price Is Right,* Lowell, 1958
*Beat the Clock,* Lowell, 1955
*2 for the Money,* Hasbro, 1955
*You Bet Your Life,* Lowell, 1955

*Charge Account,* Lowell, 1961
*$64,000 Question,* Lowell, 1955
*Break the Bank,* Bettye B, 1956
*Face the Facts,* Lowell, 1961
*Play Your Hunch,* Transogram, 1960

## TURN OUT THE LIGHTS

During the fifties and sixties, "monsters" roamed the world: communism, the Bomb—even our own government and the Establishment were out to get us. It was Us vs. Them, and even your best friend was suspect. Who knew what hideous creature he could turn into? You could pick a card and find out.

Horror and mystery games were extremely popular during this period, from the Ouija board, which offered cryptic, mostly incomprehensible mes-

sages regarding your future success or demise, to Green Ghost, the glow-in-the-dark game where lucky players reached into dark pits containing feathers, bones, or snakes (actually, rubber bands) to find small green ghosts. These games were favorites because, well, who doesn't like a good scare now and then—particularly at the expense of your little brother or sister.

## Transsogram

If you were a kid in the sixties, there was nothing like opening an enormous game box. Invariably it contained a huge piece of molded plastic—and if it glowed in the dark, all the better! Well, kids certainly weren't disappointed if they received Transogram's three-dimensional game, Green Ghost, one of the first glow-in-the-dark board games.

Designed by Transogram's Joe Wetherell, Green Ghost was one of the company's best-selling games in the sixties. "The concept of the game was actually inspired by the *spinner*," says Wetherell. "We thought a glowing green ghost would make a great spinner. The ghost's hand would point down at the number of moves, and of course we wanted it to make a scary sound."

The Toy Research Institute was Transogram's internal creative organization; the staff included game designers, artists, sculptors, and model makers. There, game ideas were fleshed out into prototypes, which were played by the staff until the kinks were worked out of the rules of play.

During the early sixties there was a strong three-dimensional trend in games. The Ideal Toy Company was doing enormously well with their 3-D games, in particular, Mouse Trap and Kaboom, so Transogram thought that might be an interesting and profitable area in which to work. Green Ghost is a product of that hunch, and it did very well for the company.

In the early 1900s, company founder Charles Raizen was a salesman for a firm that made transfer sewing patterns. (The transfers allowed you to iron sewing patterns directly onto fabric.) Raizen became so successful as a salesman that he eventually bought the company from the owner in 1914, changing its name to Transogram in reference to the transfers they made. The company backed into the toy industry when Raizen suggested they make similar transfer patterns for doll clothes.

In the late thirties, Charles Raizen was inspired by the birth of the famous Dionne Quintuplets, who were delivered by Dr. Allan Roy Dafoe, a country doctor in Canada. In response, Transogram created Little Country Doctor and Nurse Kits, which were very

*Charles Raizen,
founder of Transogram.*

*Green Ghost, Transogram, 1965*

popular with children. Later, other toy companies followed suit with similar kits.

By the 1960s Transogram had established itself in the game business and had become one of the biggest exploiters of television, scooping up an impressive array of character and program licenses, and advertising heavily on network television. More than any other game company, Transogram personified the close relationship that had developed between television and the toy industry, doing so with imaginative designs that were some of the best of the period.

**Ka-bala,** *Transogram, 1967*
*Transogram's follow-up to Green Ghost was a giant glowing take-off*
*on the Ouija board. Unfortunately, sales weren't spirited.*

Left:
**Nancy Drew Mystery Game,** Parker Bros., 1957

**Veda Board,** Pressman, 1959

**Outer Limits,** *Milton Bradley, 1964*
*This much-sought-after game contained cards that featured some of the more memorable creatures from the television series.*

**Weird-Oh's,** *Ideal, 1964*
*These grotesque but really cool little monsters had their own line of model kits, which were popular with teenage boys.*

**King Zor,** *Ideal, 1963*
*Toy inventor Marvin Glass's plastic mechanical dinosaur was inspired by the legend of St. George and the dragon. Brisk sales of the toy, however, inspired the board game.*

**King Kong,** *Ideal, 1963*
*Thirty years after the original motion picture, Ideal resurrected Kong in this board game.*

**Godzilla,** *Ideal, 1963*

**Voodoo,** *Schaper, 1967*
*Another game that had kids sticking pins in a doll. This time, wrong moves sent a little plastic Witch Doctor jumping from his hut, and you out of the game.*

**Kreskin's ESP,** *Milton Bradley, 1967*
*This nontraditional game from Milton Bradley was developed the same year Twister had its phenomenal success.*

**The Twilight Zone,** *Ideal, 1964*
*Rod Serling's genius didn't show up in this poor adaptation of the classic thought-provoking show.*

**Mystic Skull,** *Ideal, 1964*
*Parents must have loved this game; kids had to stick pins in their opponents' voodoo dolls before their own doll was filled with pins. A revolving skull determined each player's fate.*

**Haunted House,** *Ideal, 1962*
*Determined to establish themselves as the "3-D game company,"*
*Ideal took this typical one-dimensional board game submitted by an*
*outside inventor and turned it into "one big monster plastic piece,"*
*says Larry Reiner, who helped start Ideal's game division.*

COPYRIGHT KING FEATURES SYNDICATE

MANUFACTURED BY TRANSOGRAM COMPANY, INC.

## PAJAMAS AND CEREAL

Mom and Pop were snug in bed, dead to the world, while the kids were anchored in front of the television set watching their favorite cartoons.

Although Saturday and early-morning programming was usually dominated by cartoons, television in the fifties also offered live-action children's shows such as "Howdy Doody" and "The Pinky Lee Show." In the sixties, there were reruns of popular primetime family programs ("Captain Gallant of the Foreign Legion," "Roy Rogers," and "Rin Tin Tin").

A few animated programs premiered on primetime, such as "The Flintstones," "The Jetsons" (ABC's first color program in 1962), and "Jonny Quest," which became popular with adults as well as children.

Superheroes also blazed across television screens. Perhaps they were popular because Americans imagined themselves surrounded by evil brutes with designs on the Earth. Maybe these villainous masterminds had already infiltrated the very core of our democratic society. Somehow, somewhere, there

***Pinky Lee and the Runaway Frankfurters,*** *Whiting, 1954*
*Born Pincus Leff in 1916, the ex-burlesque comic was a rousing hit with kids and their moms during the run of "The Pinky Lee Show."*

must be *someone* who could save us! And if not, at least we could have fun imagining help was on the way.

Children's programming was an obvious hunting ground for idea-hungry toy companies. After all, cartoon characters, like their counterparts in live-action programs, were presold products. How could game executives go wrong? Producers and networks, in turn, were equally thrilled to sell their beloved characters to toy manufacturers. Ironically, in today's world of children's programming some series are more likely to be inspired by a preexisting, best-selling toy or game, rather than an original idea. Regardless, early-morning television belonged, and still belongs, to the realm of kids, pajamas, and breakfast cereals.

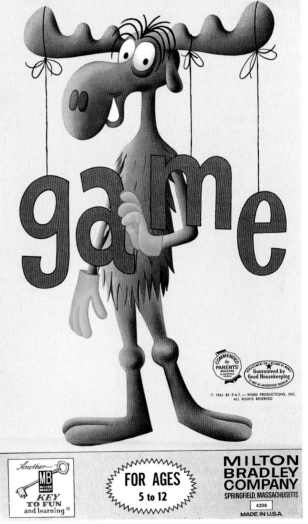

***Bullwinkle Hide and Seek,*** *Milton Bradley, 1961*
*Early in this program's history, the moose from Frostbite Falls instructed kids to pull the knobs off their TV sets to assure that they'd be on the same channel the next week. Over 20,000 kids obeyed, and their parents and NBC were furious.*

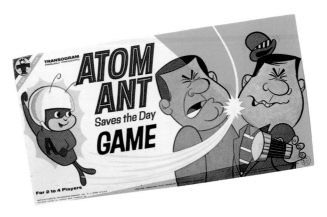

**Atom Ant,** *Transogram, 1966*

**Underdog,** *Milton Bradley, 1964*
*"When Polly's in trouble, I am not slow, it's hip, hip, hip and away I go." The voice of Wally Cox was immortalized as the canine crime-fighter.*

**Captain Kangaroo,** *Milton Bradley, 1956*
*Set in the Captain's Treasure House. A close look at the shelves reveals a couple of Milton Bradley's classic children's games.*

**Chuggedy Chug,** *Milton Bradley, 1955*
*Ride with Paul Winchell and his wooden friends Jerry Mahoney and
Knucklehead Smiff, through Jollytown to the finish line.*

**Felix the Cat,** *Milton Bradley, 1960*

**Laurel and Hardy,** Transogram, 1962
The game finds Stan and Ollie baby-sitting a couple of monkeys.

**Gumby and Pokey Playful Trails,** CO-5 Company, 1968
Art Clokey's clay puppets come to life here, where Gumby has to catch Pokey and ride him to the corral.

**Milton the Monster,** Milton Bradley, 1966

**Snagglepuss,** Transogram, 1963
"Heavens to Murgatroyd, exit stage left . . . ," and with that, the thespian lion is off to the picnic with Yogi Bear and his friends.

**The Phantom,** *Transogram, 1966*
*A man in purple tights, according to the directions, "rules the jungle, bringing peace and safety to the natives." Just as the Phantom left the mark of his ring at the scene of trouble, players left their mark stamped in clay around the game board.*

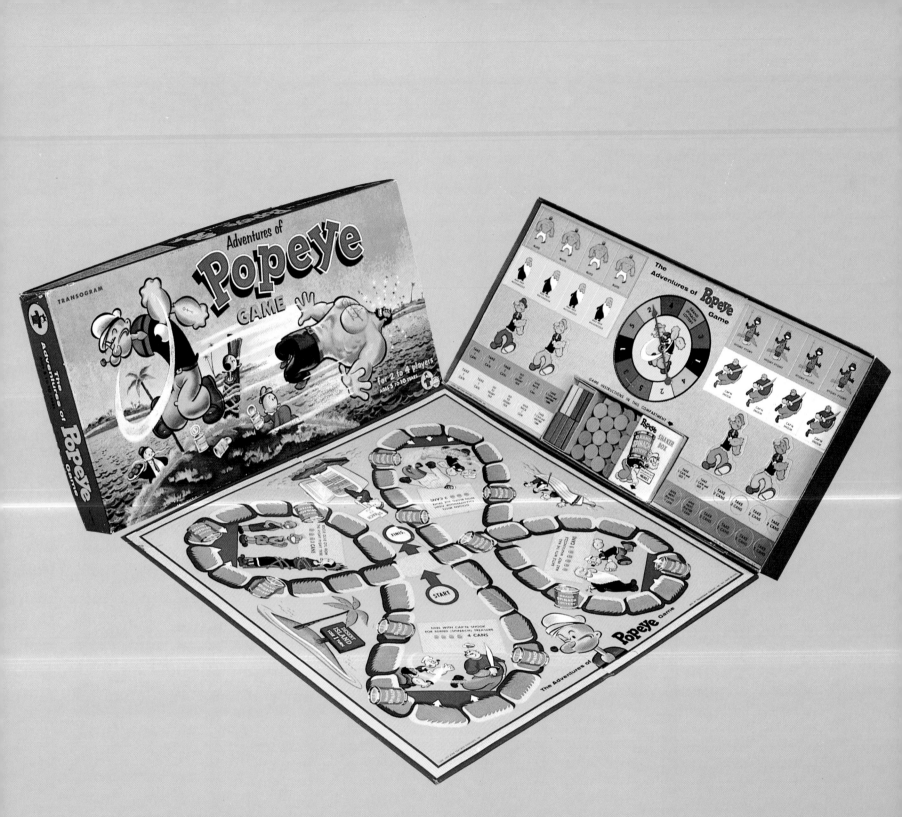

**Adventures of Popeye,** *Transogram, 1957*
*Players won by eating the right number of cans of spinach, which are won in the "Grand Spinach Lottery."*

**Calling Superman,** Transogram, 1954
Players were reporters covering stories for the Daily Planet. When danger blocked their way, they could call Superman for help.

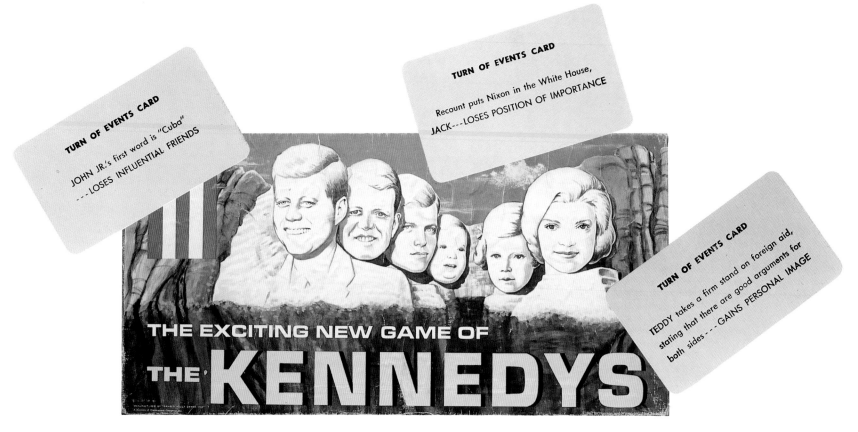

TURN OF EVENTS CARD

JOHN JR.'s first word is "Cuba"
--- LOSES INFLUENTIAL FRIENDS

TURN OF EVENTS CARD

Recount puts Nixon in the White House,
JACK---LOSES POSITION OF IMPORTANCE

TURN OF EVENTS CARD

TEDDY takes a firm stand on foreign aid,
stating that there are good arguments for
both sides --- GAINS PERSONAL IMAGE

**The Kennedys,** *Transco, 1962*
*A real live family with superhero status. Invented by two Harvard students, Jack Winter and Alfred Harrison, the game challenged players to gain complete control of the country by maintaining their personal images, gathering popular support, and avoiding political gaffes.*

**Batman,** *Milton Bradley, 1966*
*In 1966, the year of the superhero, television and game companies flooded the market with games about popular comic-book characters.*

**Captain America,** *Milton Bradley, 1966*
*The lightning-fast Captain America and his partner, Bucky, crush evil and corruption as they make their way to the Radar Lookout.*

## NO GIRLS ALLOWED!

The mere sight of sports or military and strategy games often sent girls fleeing from the clubhouse.

In the case of war games, most girls had no desire to participate in the dirty business of world conquest. Secret plotting and ambushes were the stuff of boyhood. You never knew what pestilent hordes might be surrounding the clubhouse. Military and strategy games helped prepare for the inevitable onslaught.

The assault, however, came from *parents,* who bitterly campaigned against war games, to the dismay of many a combat-ready kid. They obviously didn't know how to have a good time.

In the mid-sixties, an organization called Parents for Responsibility in the Toy Industry (composed chiefly of militant moms) picketed the American Toy Fair in New York City, protesting the proliferation of war games and toys, and citing the harmful psychological conditioning such toys were having on their children. Their signs read "Toy Fair or Warfare?" and they brought the toy industry under close scrutiny.

Even some older games, staples of the industry, came under criticism. Parker Brothers' Risk (1959) was one example. At a time when the Vietnam War was inciting protests and the foreign policy of all nations was in question, Risk, a game of world conquest, turned some heads. The object of the game was "to occupy every territory on the board and, in so doing, eliminate the other players." The criticism was that it tacitly condoned international aggression. But like most war games, it also required thoughtful strategy and provided hours of fun for kids and adults alike.

While "violence in sports" would have to wait until the seventies to fall under scrutiny, tabletop sports games remained free of controversy for obvious reasons: you couldn't break an arm or a collarbone playing an indoor sports game. They were popular because even the wimpiest kid on the block could be a professional sports figure and win that big game. Roll the dice and find out who will be the next Bart Starr.

## Hasbro

American toy buyers at Toy Fair assured Hasbro that there would be no interest in a soldier doll for boys. Boys are comfortable playing with *armies* of soldiers, they advised, but they'd perceive a single figure—particularly one that came with clothing and accessories—as a doll! Of course, the toy industry was mistaken, and Hasbro released four G.I. Joe dolls in 1964—a soldier, a Marine, a sailor, and a pilot—to extraordinary success.

The G.I. Joe action figure was originally inspired by the main character of a television show about the U.S. Marines, "The Lieutenant," but Hasbro was hesitant to wed the proposed toy with a fleeting television series. It wanted to create its own character, one it would have complete control over.

Following the lead of other companies who created board games based on toys in their product lines, Hasbro produced spin-off games inspired by its G.I. Joe characters: G.I. Joe Card Game, G.I. Joe Marine Paratrooper Game, G.I. Joe Rik-O-Shay Game, and, shown here, the G.I. Joe Infantry Game.

**G.I. Joe Combat Infantry Game,** *Hasbro, 1964*

*Four war games surround Ralph Pereida's stunning original artwork for the Ideal game based on another television war drama, "Garrison's Gorillas."*

**Battle Line,** Ideal, 1964          **P.T. Boat 109,** Ideal, 1963
**The Lieutenant,** Transogram, 1963          **Rat Patrol,** Pressman, 1967

Like many toy companies, Hasbro had a somewhat inauspicious beginning. Two Polish immigrants, brothers Henry and Hilal Hassenfeld, established their family textile business in Providence, Rhode Island, in 1923. They single-handedly created the pencil-box business when they began covering cardboard boxes with remnant fabrics. In the late thirties, they complemented their school supplies venture with modeling-clay sets and doctor and nurse kits, taking their first step into the toy business.

Hasbro's first big hit in the toy industry was the 1953 introduction of an odd little item called Mr. Potato Head (then requiring a *real* potato, not included). Mr. Potato Head was the first American toy advertised on television, and it grossed over $4 million dollars in its first year. By 1963, Mr. Potato Head was fully manufactured in plastic, and Hasbro was well on its way to becoming one of the more diversified toy manufacturers in the country.

**12 O'Clock High,** *Ideal, 1965*
When Brig. Gen. Frank Savage, played by Robert Lansing (below) was killed on the show, Ideal issued the second version of this game with the new star, Paul Burke, on the cover.

**Rat Patrol,** *Transogram, 1966*
Jumping sand dunes and kicking Nazi butt was all in a day's work for the four renegade commandos fighting in the Afrika Korps during World War II.

**Siege,** Milton Bradley, 1966

**Dogfight,** Milton Bradley, 1962
Jim Houlihan of Milton Bradley remembers a scathing letter they received from an anti–animal cruelty organization in Washington, D.C., asking how Milton Bradley could have the nerve to produce a game about dogs fighting. It was a hit, anyway.

**Sonar Sub Hunt,** *Mattel, 1961*
*Offering periscopes, flashing lights, and buzzer alarms, Mattel went all out with this elaborate simulation of a battle under the sea.*

**Rock'em Sock'em Robots,** *Marx, 1966*

*"Welcome to the heavyweight championship of the universe. In this corner, at 375 pounds, from Soltarus II, the rollicking Red Rocker. And in this corner at 382 pounds, the pride of Umgluck, the beautiful Blue Bomber. Let's fight fair, and may the best 'bot win!"*

**Pro League Basketball,** *Gotham, ca. 1960*

**Foto Electric Football,** *Cadaco-Ellis, 1950*
*After the offense and defense slid their plays into the unit, a card would slowly be removed, revealing the outcome.*

**Junior Table Top Bowling Alley,**
Merit, 1958
Start a league right in your own living
room, and you don't have to rent those
silly shoes.

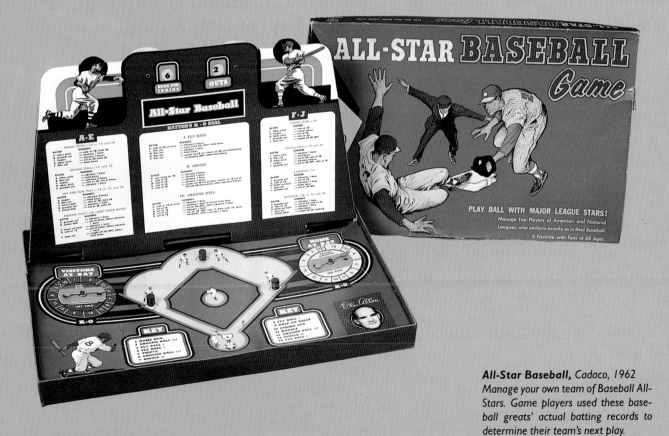

**All-Star Baseball,** Cadaco, 1962
Manage your own team of Baseball All-
Stars. Game players used these baseball greats' actual batting records to
determine their team's next play.

**American Derby,** *Cadaco-Ellis, 1950*

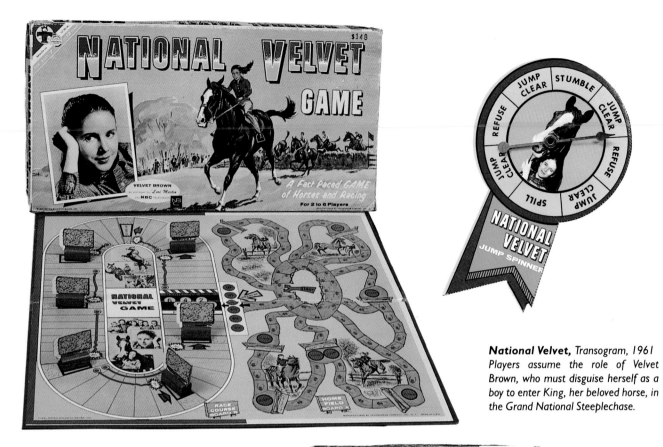

**National Velvet,** *Transogram, 1961*
*Players assume the role of Velvet Brown, who must disguise herself as a boy to enter King, her beloved horse, in the Grand National Steeplechase.*

**Speedway,** *Ideal, 1961*
One of Ideal's first games, this combined the high-speed thrills of auto racing and the carnival game of "Ring the Bell."

As kids, it seemed to us as if grown-ups were incapable of having fun; yet we all *wanted* to be grown up. Why? Because no one told adults what to do—or so we thought. Somehow, though, we realized that with freedom came immense responsibilities and untold problems. Of course, that didn't stop us. We raced into adulthood playing games that simulated real life, including the joys and problems that come with it.

Real-life games offered some semblance of control over our lives. When you're a kid, you're surrounded by a big, mysterious world. What better way to deal with its complexity than to bring it down to your level—down to a board game, in which you could become a parent, go bankrupt, or rule a superpower nation. At least until Mom called you home for supper.

## Milton Bradley—Key to Fun and Learning

In 1860, a young entrepreneur named Milton Bradley established a lithography business in Springfield, Massachusetts. One of the first works he printed was a portrait of a beardless Abraham Lincoln. Lincoln had just been nominated for the presidency and sales of the print skyrocketed—that is, until Lincoln began campaigning with his now-famous beard. Consequently, sales dropped dramatically, and Milton Bradley, now looking for other printing projects, decided to go to press with a children's parlor game he had invented earlier.

The Checkered Game of Life was a moralistic game in which good deeds were rewarded and bad ones punished, and the first player to reach "Happy Old Age" was the winner. The response to The Checkered Game of Life was so overwhelming that Bradley began to devote all his time to the production of the game.

*Milton Bradley*

*Bradley's lithograph of the beardless Lincoln*

**Life,** *Milton Bradley, 1960*

When the Civil War broke out the following year, Bradley closed his print shop and volunteered to work at the Springfield Armory. The town was flooded with Union soldiers. At night, the soldiers huddled around campfires, bored. Noticing this, Bradley designed a light, compact game kit for the soldiers containing nine games, including The Checkered Game of Life. The kit was an instant hit, and Bradley was swamped with orders. When the war ended, Milton Bradley expanded his newfound business, launching an American enterprise that has become truly legendary.

In 1960, the Milton Bradley Company celebrated its 100th anniversary. To commemorate the event, they hired inventor Reuben Klamer to come up with a centennial game for them. "While rummaging through the Milton Bradley company archives I spotted The Checkered Game of Life game board on a wall," says Reuben Klamer. "The idea occurred to me that the theme was an excellent one for a new game about 'life' and would also be an appropriate theme for their 100th anniversary promotion at Toy Fair in 1960."

Inspired, Klamer invented The Game of Life. In keeping with our modern age, the object of the game was altered: players tried to become a millionaire in order to win the game. Apparently, a "Happy Old Age" is no longer good enough.

**Leave It to Beaver Money Maker,** *Hasbro, 1959*
*"Ward, I'm worried about the Beaver—he's becoming too ambitious."*
*In spite of the title, the game begins with Dad giving each player $20.*

**Big Business,** *Transogram, 1959*
*Transogram's "blue chip" game was a staple of the company for nearly 30 years.*

**Square Mile,** *Milton Bradley, 1962*
*In this game, players are "modern age pioneers who take a square mile of raw land and develop it into a thriving community."*

**Kommissar,** *Selchow & Righter, 1966*
*One wrong move and it's—Pow!—back to the salt mines.*

**Screwball Mad Mad Game,** *Transogram, 1958*
*Transogram's wacky game about life in the advertising industry had to have a make-over when Mad Magazine threatened them with a lawsuit because the main character on the box too closely resembled Mad's mascot, Alfred E. Neuman.*

# Parker Brothers

The first American board game, Mansion of Happiness, was designed to promote good values. However, it was perceived by some kids as being *too* pious; one such youngster was George S. Parker of Salem, Massachusetts. In response, 16-year-old Parker invented his own game, Banking (1883), sans moral lecturing, simply to entertain himself and his game-playing friends. After much goading from one friend, Parker published the game himself using $40 of his $50 life savings. He sold all but a dozen of the 500 sets, making a profit of over $150. Inspired and a little bit bemused by his first success, he invented and published additional games. In 1888, he teamed up with his brother Charles and started the Parker Brothers Company.

In 1932, Charles B. Darrow, an unemployed heating engineer from Germantown, Pennsylvania, submitted a game he had invented to Parker Brothers, one of the major game manufacturers in the country. After playing the game, Parker Brothers executives cited 52 fundamental playing errors in the game play; the decision to turn it down was unanimous. Undaunted, Darrow printed 5,000 copies of the game, which he sold to the Wannamaker Company in Philadelphia and F.A.O. Schwarz in New York. When Parker Brothers heard of Darrow's sales, they reconsidered and offered him an attractive royalty contract, which he accepted. Charles B. Darrow's real estate game, Monopoly, became Parker Brothers' biggest hit.

The history of Monopoly traditionally has begun with Charles Darrow. However, variations of this real estate game existed long before Darrow submitted his version to Parker Brothers. In 1904, Elizabeth Magie Phillips invented The Landlord's Game, which demonstrated (some say *advocated*) the principles of the single tax—in this case, on real estate. The game's rules were quite similar to Monopoly. Players attempted to gain wealth by buying and selling real estate that included railroads, utilities, and properties (named after streets).

When Parker Brothers attempted to patent Monopoly in 1934, they were reminded of Magie Phillips's The Landlord's Game, a game that the company had considered and declined ten years earlier. To protect their new investment, Parker Brothers immediately offered to buy Magie Phillips's patent. She agreed, provided that Parker Brothers produce and distribute her game also, which they did.

Another variation is a game manufactured in the early thirties by Knapp Electric Company, called Finance. Invented by Dan Layman (a student who had played Magie Phillips's game in college), Finance employed familiar Monopoly devices: Community Chest cards, Chance cards, Free Parking, and Go to Jail.

Even more similar in design was an unpublished game called Atlantic City Monopoly invented by Ruthie Thorp Harvey, a Quaker woman who lived in Atlantic City, New Jersey. In 1930, Miss Harvey handpainted her game boards on oilcloth. Her intention was simply to provide fun and entertainment for her family and friends. She had no intention of professionally selling the games. Surprisingly, her boards were very similar in design to Darrow's and the version we play today. Properties were grouped by color around the outer edge of the board representing the playing path, and each was named after a street in her hometown of Atlantic City. (Evidence suggests that Darrow had been exposed to this version through an old friend of his wife's.)

It's difficult to say how much of Monopoly was actually Charles Darrow's own invention. In the future, perhaps the world will be thanking Darrow, Elizabeth Magie Phillips, *and* Ruthie Thorp Harvey for the game of Monopoly.

Although Parker Brothers is home to other classic games such as Sorry!, Clue, and Risk, Monopoly remains its most well-known and best-selling game. It's printed in 23 languages and is generally translated into the respective foreign country's real estate and currency. In England, Boardwalk and Park Place become London's Mayfair and Park Lane. In France, Boardwalk is rue de la Paix.

Since its introduction, Monopoly has been a virtual phenomenon, inspiring national and worldwide tournaments, marathons (in elevators, in trees, underwater), and giant indoor and outdoor reproductions of the game board. When Atlantic City threatened to

**Monopoly,** *Parker Bros.*
*Marvin Gardens is the only property on the board not named after an Atlantic City street, but rather an elite community a few miles away correctly spelled Marven Gardens.*

change the names of two of its streets—Baltic and Mediterranean avenues—the Monopoly-loving public was outraged and protested the proposal. Parker Brothers' own president, Edward Parker, addressed the city commissioners in an eloquent plea to save Baltic and Mediterranean avenues. The proposal was voted down, preserving two landmarks that Parker Brothers had made famous.

**Astron,** *Parker Bros., 1955*
An intercontinental jet race. The company changed the name to Sky Lanes a year later because it was more representational of the game's concept.
The original name seemed to imply space travel.

**Scoop,** *Parker Bros., 1954*
*Exercise your First Amendment rights and become the next William Randolph Hearst in this newspaper-editing game. A unique dial telephone gives you instructions from your editor.*

**NO BOYS ALLOWED!**

Let's face it: when we were growing up, games about teen life catered almost exclusively to girls. Mystery Date, Miss Popularity, and other games were designed to fuel a teenage girl's social fantasies, but there was nothing quite the same for boys, who were too busy destroying battleships and performing other intrepid deeds while playing games.

During the 1960s, designing games especially for girls was a delicate business. The problem was how to appeal to girls' fantasies without drawing criticism from the growing women's liberation movement. Liberation or not, many such games did very well. Really now, what could be more important than the dreamy new high-school football quarterback or, even more important, who he was taking to the prom?!

Through games about teen life, girls could overcome adolescent feelings of awkwardness and insecu-rity and have a second chance at going to the prom with Billy or Johnny—or a third chance, or a fourth—all in one afternoon.

## "You Can Tell It's Mattel—It's Swell!"

Everyone said that a doll with breasts would never sell: kids prefer *baby* dolls, and, besides, parents wouldn't allow a buxom doll in their home. But Ruth Handler, president of Mattel Toys in 1959, noticed that as her daughter grew older, she preferred playing with paper dolls because they generally depicted teenage or adult characters, role models to which she aspired. And, like all paper dolls, these characters had change-able clothes.

**Mystery Date,** *Milton Bradley, 1965*
*Milton Bradley received complaints from mothers who resented the portrayal of the "loser date" (a dirty, disheveled young man). Their complaint: "My son looks and dresses like that, and there's nothing wrong with him!" A few years later, the mystery dates' photographs were changed to homogenized illustrations.*

This inspired Mattel to create an adult fashion model doll with clothes and accessories. Their 11½-inch-tall doll Barbie (named after the owners' daughter; Ken was named after their son), proved a skeptical toy industry wrong and took the world by storm in 1959.

Mattel began in a Hawthorne, California, garage in 1945. At the time, original founders Harold Matson and Elliot Handler manufactured doll furniture. They coined their company name by combining letters of their last and first names, respectively. Later, Matson sold his half of the partnership, and Elliot Handler and his wife Ruth reigned over the business.

Mattel became the first toy company to advertise *year-round* on network television; they were a sponsor for the 1955 television show, "The Mickey Mouse Club." (The toy industry traditionally had relied on seasonal marketing). It proved so successful that other companies followed suit.

Although toy companies were rapidly exploiting popular television shows, they sometimes turned to their own product lines for board game ideas. In Mattel's case, what better inspiration than its most lucrative item in the sixties: Barbie. Barbie World of Fashion, Barbie's Keys to Fame, and, shown here, Barbie—Queen of the Prom were Mattel games that vied for young girls' attention. Chatty Cathy was another Mattel doll that inspired a board game. (Other companies used the same strategy; Ideal created board games based on several of its popular play toys: Mr. Machine, King Zor the Dinosaur, and Pattie Playpal, among others).

Although Mattel was never completely successful in the game market, it was and still is a major force in the toy industry.

Previous page:

**Barbie, Queen of the Prom,** Mattel, 1960

*Mattel promoted this as a game with real-life appeal. What could be more realistic? All you had to do was to become president of a school club, buy the right evening dress with your meager allowance and the baby-sitting money you'd saved, get a steady boyfriend, and, that's it, you win!*

**Tammy,** Ideal, 1963
**Gidget,** Standard Toykraft, 1965
**Gidget Fortune Teller Game,** Milton Bradley, 1966
*Here are three games that show the female teenager in her natural habitat: on the phone!*

**Margie,** *Milton Bradley, 1961*
*This series starring Cynthia Pepper lasted only one season and focused on teen life in the Roaring Twenties.*

**Twiggy,** *Milton Bradley, 1967*
*Milton Bradley hopped on the Mod bandwagon with this game about the 91-pound model but soon realized her popularity had been as short as her skirts.*

**Shindig,** *Remco, 1965*
*The teen music show hosted by Jimmy O'Neill spawned this entertainment trivia game.*

**The Monkees,** *Transogram, 1967*

**Beatles, Flip Your Wig,** *Milton Bradley, 1964*

*The Beatles' instant popularity took everyone by such surprise that Milton Bradley's Jim Houlihan and his staff had only three weeks before the annual Toy Fair convention to invent a game based on the hit group. In fact, they created the rules so quickly that when the artwork was returned to them, they discovered they had forgotten how to play the game! Despite the Beatles' great success, no other games were developed about the band.*

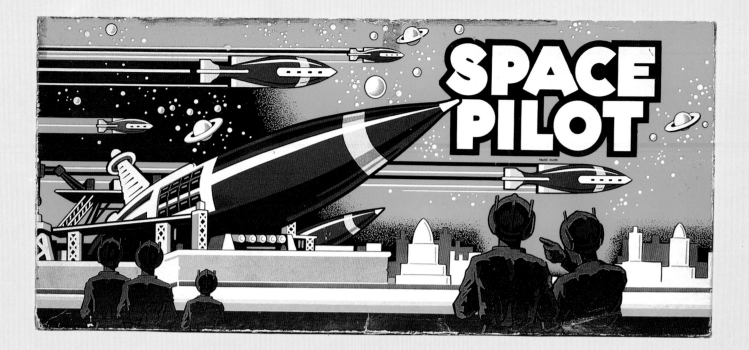

## 3-2-1-BLASTOFF

Although the public was preoccupied with Western heroes in the fifties, a new frontier began to draw attention, inhabited by brand-new heroes: space explorers! Science fiction and fantasy were seeping into books and television programming. Consequently, toy companies began marketing outer-space toys and games. While science fiction fired our imaginations, it also planted a seed of apprehension: who or what else was "out there?"

The Milton Bradley Company was pleased when it managed to tie up a string of space-based licenses in 1953 as inspiration for upcoming board games. Unfortunately, American moms (who, after all, were the ones who purchased games for their kids) overlooked the wonders of space, latching onto its potential menace instead. Mothers ignored them, so space games never left the launchpad in stores.

"No mother wants her little boy to be a space man," theorizes James J. Shea (then president of Milton Bradley) in his book *It's All in the Game*. "She'll go along with his being a cowboy or a private detective or any number of other things. But a space man never. Outer space is just too far for him to travel from home and mother."

It wasn't until the launch of the first *real* satellite, the Soviet Union's Sputnik in 1957, that the public finally embraced outer-space merchandise. Suddenly, space exploration was no longer a fantasy; it was necessary for the very survival of our country. Subsequent NASA space missions supplied some real-life heroes to fuel our imaginations: *astronauts*. Now, blasting off into the great unknown was the patriotic thing to do. And how could Mom object to that? Besides, these new "space men" were so clean-cut and handsome. Why, they could be your next door neighbors.

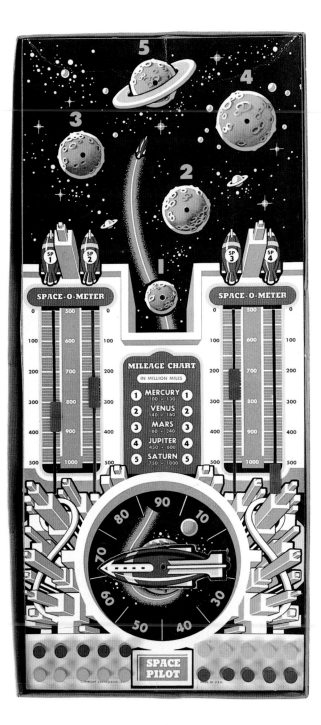

**Orbit,** *Parker Bros., 1959*

**Buck Rogers,** *Transogram, circa 1965*

**Leave It to Beaver Rocket to the Moon,** *Hasbro, 1959*

**Star Trek,** *Ideal, 1966*
*Although the television program was doing poorly in the ratings, Mr. Julie Cooper, Ideal's head of research and development, invented and released this game anyway.*

**Space Pilot,** *Cadaco-Ellis, 1951*
*This gorgeous box and game board depict interplanetary travel in the future.*

**Captain Video,** *Milton Bradley, 1950*
*The prop budget for this network series was $50 a week. The show was extremely low tech, but kids ate it up. Milton Bradley's game recreated an instrument panel of a spaceship for piloting your ship to Dr. Pauli's evil laboratory.*

**Steve Scott Space Scout,** *Transogram, 1951*
*Charles Raizen, president of Transogram, named this space hero after his newborn grandson, Steven Scott Fadem.*

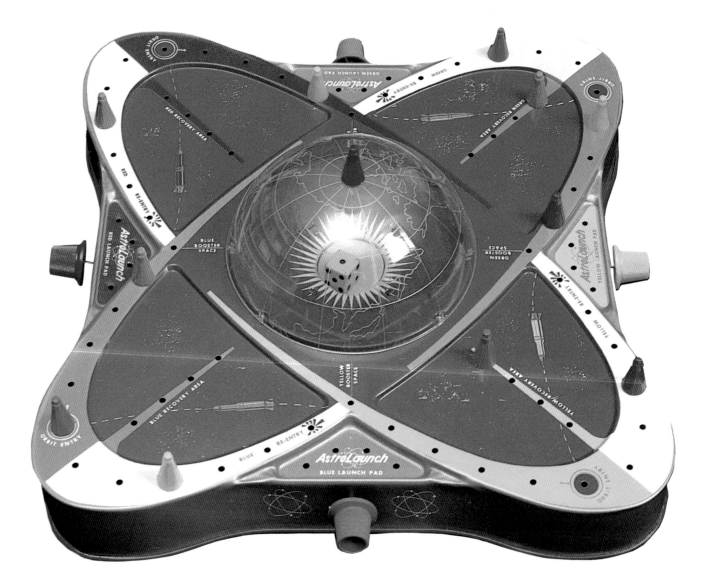

**Astro Launch,** *Ohio Art, 1963*
*The company famous for Etch-A-Sketch released this tin wonder. Moves were determined by a die that was "launched" within a translucent plastic globe.*

**Lost in Space,** *Milton Bradley, 1965*
*The Robinson family finds itself in trouble again with the ferocious Cyclops.*

Perhaps the best-selling detection-and-deduction game of all time is Parker Brothers' Clue. Originally a British game, Clue took America by storm in the fifties and is still popular today. Later mystery games followed the path of most other games, incorporating television programs as their themes.

The mid-fifties brought Sgt. Joe Friday, Officer Gannon, and actual Los Angeles police cases into our living rooms; and if the family didn't like the way Friday and Gannon solved crimes, they could try it themselves with Transogram's board game Dragnet, one of several games based on the series. Other popular television crime-fighting shows of the sixties included "Perry Mason," "The FBI," and "77 Sunset Strip," all of which made it to the game board.

**Clue,** *Parker Brothers, 1956*
*The most popular "whodunit" in game history.*

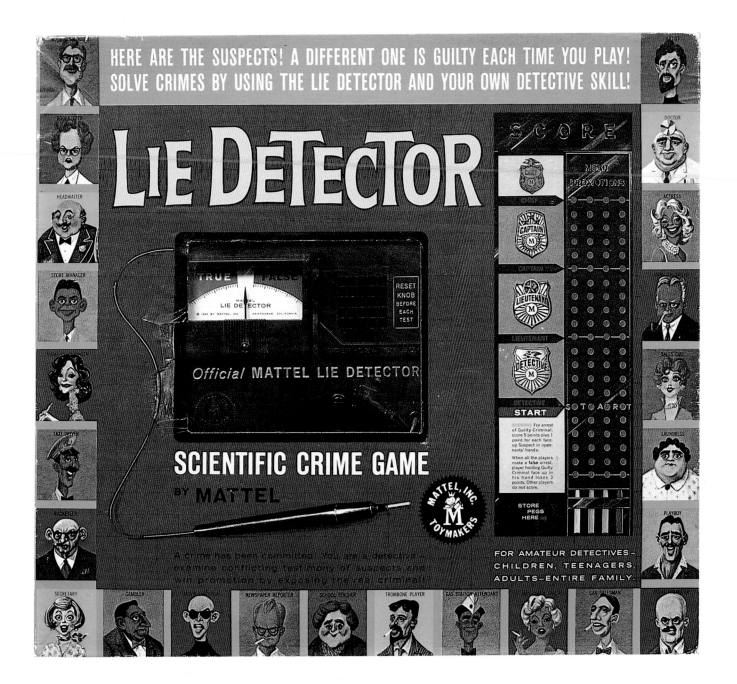

**Lie Detector,** *Mattel, 1960*
*An ingenious game with 24 comical suspects, one of them a criminal. Slip your suspect card into the lie detector and listen for the bell, the sign of a liar.*

**Dragnet,** Transogram, 1955
**Perry Mason,** Transogram, 1959
Both games were nearly identical; only the names and cards were changed to protect the innocent.

**Philip Marlowe,** Transogram, 1960

**FBI,** *Transogram, 1961*
*In the shadow of the Capitol building, two FBI agents use the latest in high-tech equipment to solve interstate crimes. Comparing fingerprints, tire-tread prints, fragments of glass, heel prints, ballistics, handwriting, and other clues, players pieced a case together like a jigsaw puzzle.*

**77 Sunset Strip,** *Lowell, 1959*
*Three handsome detectives on the beat in sunny Los Angeles.*

**Peter Gunn,** *Lowell, 1960*

**Surfside 6,** Lowell, 1962
Three handsome detectives on the beat in sunny Miami Beach. Sound familiar?

## DISNEY'S WORLD

Disneyland is the utopia of amusement parks: the self-proclaimed "Happiest Place on Earth." From the dusty yet paved "trails" of Frontierland to the snowcapped peak of the Matterhorn, Disneyland is a microcosm of the world, real and imaginary.

The park and its rides have been the inspiration for board games since it opened. The Disneyland Game produced by Rand McNally in 1955 was the most ambitious, a large tin lithographed Disneyland globe with each hemisphere showing two "lands" from the park. The playing pieces were magnetic Disney characters that traveled around the world as if held by gravity.

Later, Transogram released a game titled simply Disneyland. The game board was a map of the park populated by famous Disney characters, including one new one: Davy Crockett. Parker Brothers released the Davy Crockett Frontierland game the same year. This was the first game based on a single "land" in the park.

Davy Crockett, played by Fess Parker, appeared on three episodes of the ABC "Disneyland" show, after which the character's popularity grew enormously. Unfortunately, the third episode was titled "Davy Crockett at the Alamo," and everyone knows what happened there. Davy let his guard down, bought the farm, and went up to that big bunkhouse in the sky, causing much distress to Disney executives who found themselves in the middle of a full-fledged craze with nowhere to go.

Around the same time, Parker Brothers released a game for each of the remaining three "lands:" Adventureland, Tomorrowland, and Fantasyland. Originally sold throughout the park for $1 each, these games allowed players to visit their Disney friends as often as they liked without spending a fortune on "E" tickets.

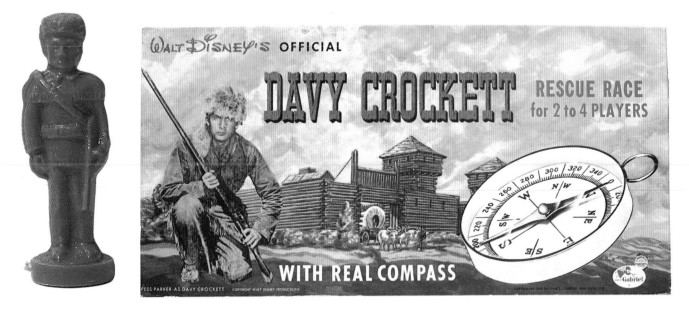

**Davy Crockett Rescue Race,** *Gabriel, 1955*

**Davy Crockett Frontierland,** *Parker Bros., 1955*
*The original Disneyland Frontierland game. After Davy's popularity faded, Parker Bros. replaced Fess Parker with a generic frontier scout and changed the box and instructions to have nothing to do with Mr. Crockett.*

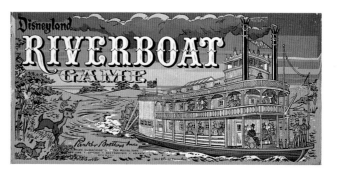

*Parker Bros. crammed the "Happiest Place on Earth" into a few small boxes.*

**Adventureland,** Parker Bros., 1956

**Fantasyland,** Parker Bros., 1956

**Monorail,** Parker Bros., 1960

**Frontierland,** Parker Bros., 1955

**Riverboat,** Parker Bros., 1960

**Tomorrowland,** Parker Bros., 1956

***Tomorrowland,*** Parker Bros., 1956

**Wonderful World of Color,** *Whitman, 1961*
Disney's new show introduced the world to Professor Ludwig Von Drake, who was the host for this game. The first player to get all of the Disney characters in his or her TV was the winner.

**Disneyland,** *Whitman, 1965*
*Take a spin on the Rocket to the Moon ride and determine your board moves at the same time. Whitman released this game in association with the park's tenth anniversary.*

**Mickey Mouse Club,** *Whitman, 1955.*
*Set smack dab in the middle of Disneyland, this game didn't feature the Mouseketeers but rather Minnie, Donald, and a couple of their lesser-known friends.*

**Zorro,** *Whitman, 1959*
*In 1957 this masked avenger stole Davy Crockett's title as the most popular television character in the country. Children abandoned their coonskin caps for the allure of a black mask and cape, and Zorro's trademark, the letter Z, began appearing everywhere.*

## WEE FOLK

Since mothers were the principal buyers of board games in the fifties and sixties (and still are), it fell on them to make the best choices for their younger children, searching for the games that their children could best understand and that would, with any luck, occupy them for hours. In a way, games were like baby-sitters, only better because they were always at your beck and call.

The key to a successful children's game is that it can be easily understood without requiring a lot of reading. One such game is Uncle Wiggley (1918), invented by Howard R. Garis, a New Jersey newspaperman and author of the syndicated "Uncle Wiggley" stories for adults and children. His inspiration came from a most peculiar situation.

While unwrapping some meat from a butcher shop, Garis noticed a curious pattern on the blood-stained paper. Intrigued, he grabbed a pencil and drew the hazardous path that his Uncle Wiggley character would have to traverse on his way to Dr. Possum's house. From there he created a simple game for children, which he took (stained butcher's paper under his arm) to the Milton Bradley Company. There, he played the game with some executives, who loved it. Little did they know that they were on their way to producing one of the most popular children's games in game history.

Cootie, Candy Land, and Chutes and Ladders are other classic children's games that have been played for generations. They are perennial best-sellers, because kids grow up to buy them for their own children. A game company couldn't ask for more than that.

***Little Rascals Bingo,*** *Gabriel, 1955*
*Join Spanky, Alfalfa, Buckwheat, and the rest of the gang for a round of bingo in their clubhouse.*

PLAYER TURNS CRANK Ⓐ WHICH ROTATES GEARS Ⓑ CAUSING LEVER Ⓒ TO MOVE AND PUSH STOP SIGN AGAINST SHOE Ⓓ. SHOE TIPS BUCKET HOLDING METAL BALL Ⓔ. BALL ROLLS DOWN RICKETY STAIRS Ⓕ AND INTO RAIN-PIPE Ⓖ WHICH LEADS IT TO HIT HELPING HAND ROD Ⓗ. THIS CAUSES BOWLING BALL Ⓘ TO FALL FROM TOP OF HELPING HAND ROD THROUGH THING-A-MA-JIG Ⓙ AND BATHTUB, Ⓚ TO LAND ON DIVING BOARD Ⓛ WEIGHT OF BOWLING BALL CATAPULTS DIVER Ⓜ THROUGH THE AIR AND RIGHT INTO WASH TUB Ⓝ CAUSING CAGE Ⓞ TO FALL FROM TOP OF POST Ⓟ AND TRAP UNSUSPECTING MOUSE.

**Mouse Trap,** *Ideal, 1963*
*Inspired by the drawings of Rube Goldberg, this was Marvin Glass's and Ideal's biggest selling game.*

## "It's a Wonderful Game—It's Ideal!"

In 1902, Morris Michtom, owner of a small toy shop in Brooklyn, New York, noticed a political cartoon in the newspaper entitled "Drawing the Line in Mississippi." The cartoon depicted President Theodore Roosevelt protecting a bear cub in the wilderness. It seems that while tending to some political problems in Mississippi, Roosevelt decided to take in some hunting. When a bear cub wandered into his camp, Roosevelt refused to shoot it and ordered the other men to let the cub wander back into the woods.

Inspired by Roosevelt's compassion, Michtom and his wife sewed together two small bears, which they displayed in their store window along with the cartoon. After receiving several offers for the cuddly bears, Michtom sent one of them to President Roosevelt, requesting permission to name them after him. The president's written reply was characteristically up-front. "I doubt that my name will mean much in the toy business, but you may use it if you wish."

The Teddy Bear was a huge success and marked the beginning of the Ideal Toy and Novelty Company in 1907.

Decades later, after a string of other successful dolls, Ideal established itself in the board game business with an unusual contraption called Mouse Trap. Inspired by Rube Goldberg's chain-reaction gizmos, Mouse Trap was invented by maverick toy inventor Marvin Glass of Chicago. Glass had originally proposed it as a toy, but Lionel Weintraub, then president of Ideal, suggested they convert it into a board game. The game was so popular, Ideal followed it up with two other three-dimensional games, Crazy Clock and Fish Bait.

Like many toy manufacturers, Ideal advertised heavily on television. For their commercials they adopted as their "mascot" one of their most popular toys in the sixties, Mr. Machine (another Marvin Glass invention, which inspired a Mr. Machine game). At the close of Ideal's television commercials, the translucent wind-up robot walked onto the screen and announced, "It's a wonderful Game—it's Ideal!" Most kids would agree.

**Little Noddy's Taxi Game,** *Parker Brothers, 1956*
*Based on characters by British children's author Enid Blyton. Kids collected nickels by driving characters like Bert the Monkey and Mr. Big Ears in their taxis around Ice Cream Town. We don't know why they needed money, since all the ice cream in town was free!*

**Merry Milkman,** *Hasbro, 1954*

*A three-player game where kids perform the duties of a milkman. Special rules allow for a fourth player, who acts as "plant manager" in charge of setting up the dairy platform (big deal!) and placing products on the other players' trucks (wow!). The rules insist that every player must be the "plant manager" at least once.*

**Pinhead,** *Remco, 1963*
A truly baffling game. The first player to reach the hiding pinhead wins. First off, why a pinhead? And why is he hiding in an open hallway? Why is the boy on the cover a giant? And why—

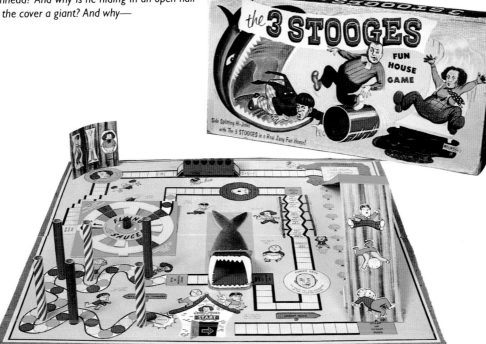

*Opposite page:*
**Cootie,** *Schaper, 1950*
Invented by ex-barber W. H. Schaper.
We're afraid to say what inspired him.

**The Three Stooges Fun House,** *Lowell, 1959*
Make your way with Moe, Larry, and Curly through this elaborate amusement-park funhouse. But watch out for the closing jaws of Moby Dick!

**Shmo,** *Remco, 1959*
Humility reigned when kids rolled out this game. After landing on certain "stupid" squares, they were instructed to perform silly stunts.

**The Game of Yertle,** *Revell, 1960*
Based on Dr. Seuss's interpretation of the Tower of Babel, the player had to balance turtles on three precarious platforms.

**Let's Face It,** *Hasbro, ca. 1955*
*Complete the faces of archetypal Americans: the cowboy, the "dude," and the fireman.*

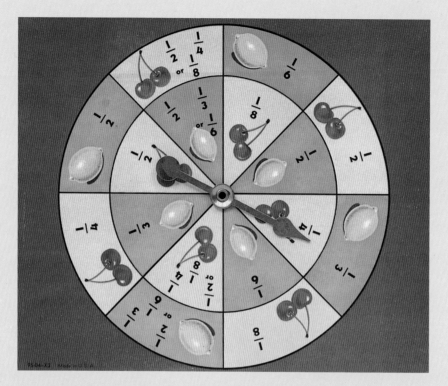

## MR. KNOW-IT-ALL

There was nothing worse than having to sit behind one of the brightest kids in your class. His or her arm would shoot up to answer every question, eclipsing your own plea (on the scant occasions you actually *knew* the answer), and singling you out when the teacher noticed the unusually quiet boy or girl sitting *behind* "Mr. Know-It-All."

So, you didn't study as much as you should—you were too busy playing games! And then your grades dropped and Mom and Dad starting buying you *educational* games—*yecch!* But, hey, they weren't so bad after all. Some of them were actually pretty cool—

Mentor, Think-A-Tron, Mr. Brain—even the names were enticing.

One of the first battery-operated educational games was Bell of Fortune (1894), which rang a bell each time a player gave the correct answer to a question. Children of the late 1800s would have been horrified by the 1961 game Mentor, with its menacing golden head. But kids of the mid-20th century demanded more visceral stimuli to satiate their short attention spans. And game companies were happy to comply, producing these imaginative sleights-of-hand to get a child to learn a thing or two.

**Ant Farm Game,** Uncle Milton, Inc., 1969
Meet the ant. Using tweezers, players moved tiny lifelike ants through their underground colony.

**Go to the Head of the Class,** Milton Bradley, 1960

**GEO-graphy,** *Cadaco-Ellis, 1957*
*The box cover makes it appear as if the continents were giant gondolas, although this educational game had nothing to do with continental drift.*

**Game of the States,** *Milton Bradley, 1960*
*Buy and sell from coast to coast as you learn about state capitols and natural resources.*

**Garroway's Game of Possession,** *Reco, 1955*
*Former NBC page Dave Garroway, who went on to host the "Today Show," lent his name to this unusual game where players bought and sold entire states.*

**Think-A-Tron,** *Hasbro, 1960*
*You were the envy of your block if you got this "machine that thinks like a man." Besides flashing lights and turning gears, it came with a memory and an assortment of punch cards to test your knowledge.*

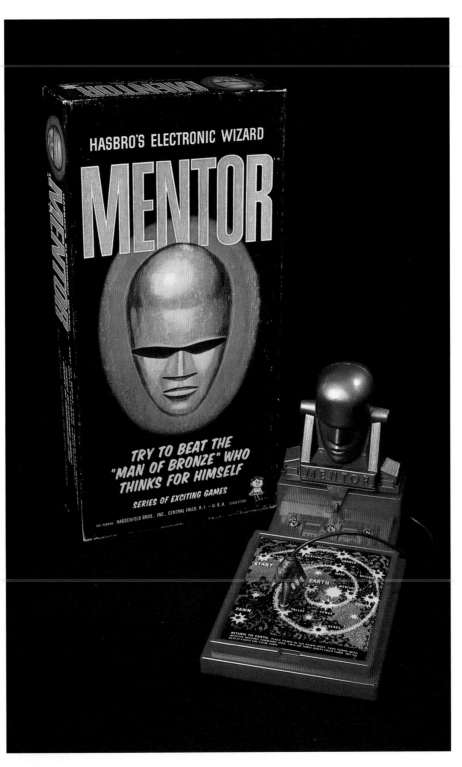

**Mentor,** *Hasbro, 1961*
*Hasbro's Mentor, who resembled the Wizard of Oz, dared you to challenge him.*

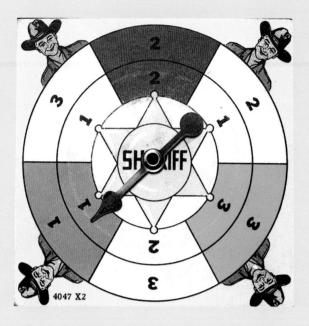

## HOWDY, PARDNER!

In the 1950s, Americans came down with an acute case of Western-itis. By 1955, Davy Crockett had single-handedly captured the entire nation, inspiring over 500 merchandising items, from toys and games to clothing (mainly coonskin caps).

The Western trend continued in the late fifties with the emergence of TV adult Westerns such as "Gunsmoke" and "Bonanza." At one time during this period more than 30 primetime Westerns were broadcast in the same season.

Perhaps Americans' fascination with Westerns during these times of uncertainty (the Cold War, the Vietnam War) was due, in part, to the need to reinforce their belief in law and order. Westerns, and the board games they inspired, offered a familiar setting, with familiar rules of conduct.

*Ross Martin shows off his personal copy of The Wild Wild West Game by Transogram.*

**Gene Autry's Dude Ranch,** *Built Rite, 1956*
*The legendary singing cowboy was "back in the saddle again" when this was released. (For some reason the flip side of the game board was a stock-car race game that had nothing to do with Westerns or Gene Autry.)*

**Branded,** *Milton Bradley, 1966*
*After being the lone survivor of a fierce battle, ex-cavalryman Chuck Connors was branded a coward. The show and the game both had the main character trying to remove this stigma by constantly proving his bravery.*

**Johnny Ringo,** *Transogram, 1960*

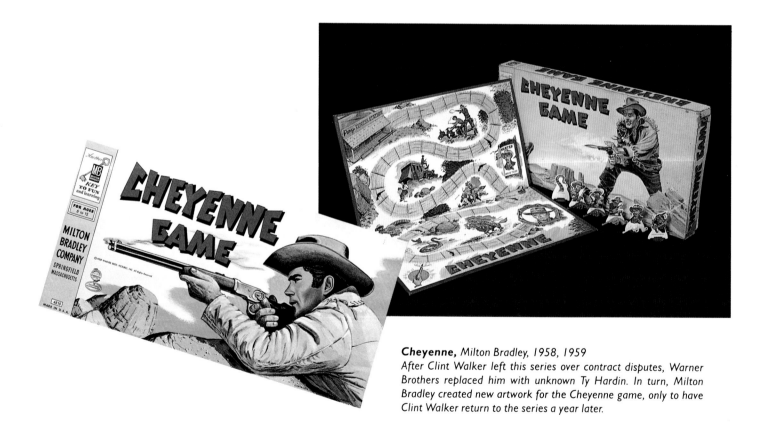

**Cheyenne,** *Milton Bradley, 1958, 1959*
*After Clint Walker left this series over contract disputes, Warner Brothers replaced him with unknown Ty Hardin. In turn, Milton Bradley created new artwork for the Cheyenne game, only to have Clint Walker return to the series a year later.*

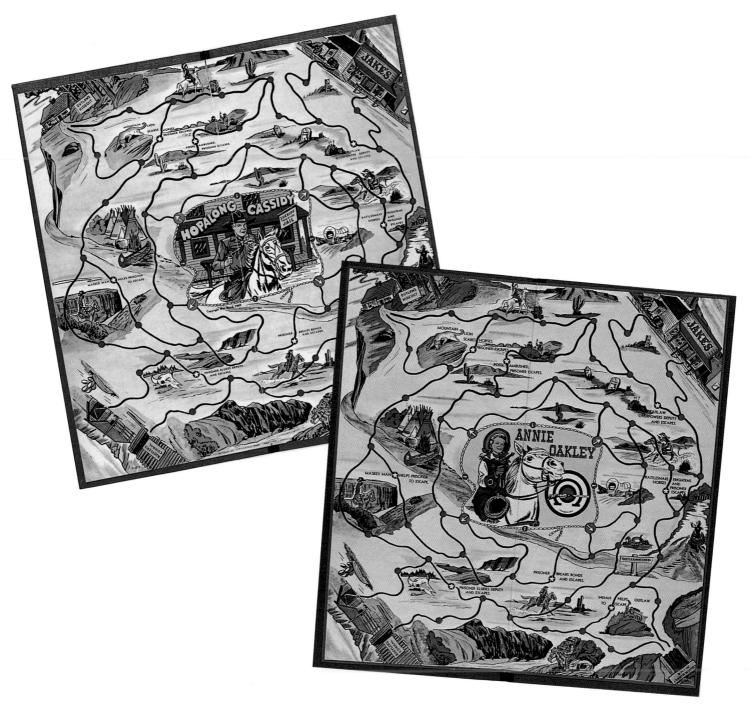

**Hopalong Cassidy,** *Milton Bradley, 1950*
*Milton Bradley president James Shea met with Hoppy, and by the end of the day had the go-ahead for this game, the first to be based on a television character.*

**Annie Oakley,** *Milton Bradley, 1958*
*Almost a decade after Milton Bradley released its Hopalong Cassidy game, it used the exact same game board for this Western starring rodeo performer Gail Davis.*

**Bat Masterson,** *Lowell, 1958*
*This game featured Tombstone, Arizona, rendered in cardboard. Between his gambling and his visits to the haberdashery, Bat tried to fill up the jail with as many outlaws as he could.*

**Gunsmoke,** *Lowell, 1958*
*TV's longest-running Western inspired this game in which Indians could be killed, but cowboys were "captured." The odds of winning the game were slightly in favor of the cowboys.*

**The Virginian,** *Transogram, 1962*
**Wagon Train,** *Milton Bradley, 1960*
**Cowboy Roundup,** *Parker Bros., 1952*
**Rin Tin Tin,** *Transogram, 1955*

**Lancer,** *Remco, 1968*
**Tales of the Texas Rangers,** *All Fair, 1956*
**Rifleman,** *Milton Bradley, 1959*
**Doc Holliday,** *Transogram, 1960*
**Stoney Burke,** *Transogram, 1963*

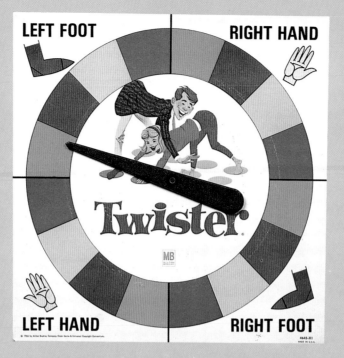

## ALL THUMBS

Good hand-eye coordination was essential in playing skill-and-action games. Although they reached full bloom in the mid-sixties, games of dexterity have always existed in various forms throughout game history.

Parker Brothers introduced its first skill-and-action game in 1897, a British game called Pillow-Dex. A precursor to Ping-Pong, Pillow-Dex had players seated at a table batting a balloon, trying to keep it from touching the table or the ground (something people tend to do when there's a loose balloon in the room). Following that was Tiddledy Winks, a game released by several companies. Parker Brothers released the first indoor tennis game, Ping-Pong, which became one of the first game crazes of the 1900s.

The skill-and-action games of the sixties were popular, in part, because they were visually stimulating. They typically employed big, unwieldy pieces of colorful plastic with moving parts; some had lights and

noisy buzzers, and most were harbingers of the video games of the seventies.

Milton Bradley's competitors accused them of selling "sex in a box" when they released the phenomenally successful action game Twister in 1966. Twister was the first game in history to use the human body as a full-fledged playing piece, and, admittedly, the Milton Bradley Company released the game with a fair amount of hesitation.

The company's fear of public criticism and its own skepticism about its potential for success were obliterated when Johnny Carson demonstrated the game on the "Tonight Show." And it didn't hurt matters that Eva Gabor, wearing a low-cut gown, was one of Johnny's guests that night.

With Eva splayed out on all fours on the polka-dot vinyl mat, Johnny twirled the spinner and took his turn. When he climbed on top of Eva, the studio audience went into hysterics, screaming and laughing.

Milton Bradley executives knew immediately they had a huge hit on their hands. More than three million copies of Twister were sold during its first year of release.

Skill-and-action games were popular because they intrigued both adults and children. They satisfied a kid's natural tendency to be hyperactive, and made a unique addition to adult parties—after all, grown-ups need to have fun, too.

**Grab a Loop,** *Milton Bradley, 1968*
*Milton Bradley's follow-up to Twister. Its object was the opposite of its predecessor: players had to stay away from each other to protect their colored loops.*

**Limbo Legs,** *Milton Bradley, 1969*
*Milton Bradley's head of research and development, Jim Houlihan, felt obligated to buy this game from an independent inventor after he tried to play it and fell on top of it, crushing the inventor's only prototype. "I smashed it to smithereens. The guy was horrified. I felt so sorry for him; I had to buy it."*

**Time Bomb,** *Milton Bradley, 1965*
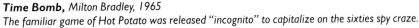
*The familiar game of Hot Potato was released "incognito" to capitalize on the sixties spy craze.*

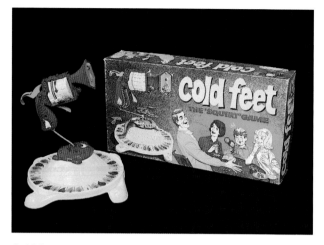

**Cold Feet,** Ideal, 1967
Larry Reiner, who headed Ideal's game division in the sixties, admits this game was simply a variation on Russian roulette. Concerned that parents might realize this, Ideal designed the gun as a nonintimidating fanciful blunderbuss.

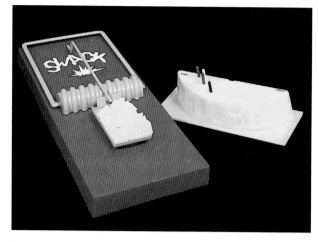

**Swack,** Ideal, 1968
Ideal reinvents the mousetrap. Kids had to remove pieces of cheese without getting their little hands caught in the trap.

**Tip It,** Ideal, 1965
Test your skill and dexterity by keeping the wacky acrobat on his perch.

**Flintstones Just for Kicks Game,** Transogram, 1962
Whack Fred on his head and watch him boot rocks into the dinosaur caves for points.

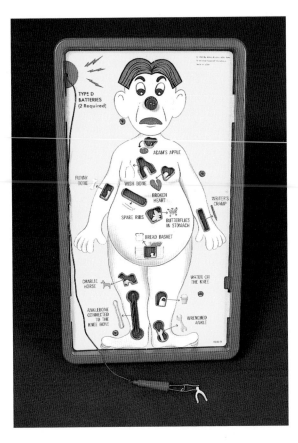

**Operation,** *Milton Bradley, 1965*
*Worried about the seriousness of the subject matter, Milton Bradley designers made the patient as cartoonlike as possible.*

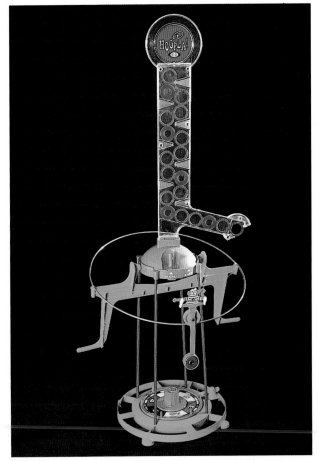

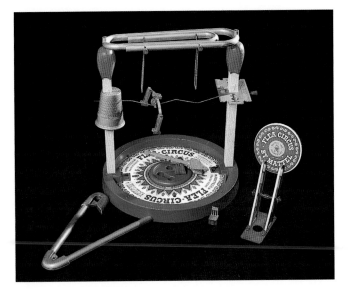

**Flea Circus,** *Mattel, 1964*
*Join a troupe of magnetic fleas as they perform death-defying feats to win the game.*

**Hoopla,** *Ideal, 1966*
*Ideal's skill game borrows from the tradition of grabbing the brass ring off a carousel.*